To What Degree

A Poet's Life Ignited

Rapheal DeAngelo

H.B. Creations
Chicago, IL 2016

Copyright © 2016 by Rapheal De'Angelo Hayden

All rights reserved. This book or any portion thereof may not be reproduced or used in any manner whatsoever without the express written permission of the publisher except for the use of brief quotations in a book review.

Printed in the United States of America

First Printing, 2016

ISBN 978-0-578-18648-1

Hayden Bros. Creations
Chicago, IL

www.rdeangelo.com

"She lit my soul in the night, I fueled the flame to her heart.
They said we had burning passion, we called it Love with a spark."

Introduction

To what degree do you feel what you feel? This collection of poetry is a culmination of life encounters and their extremes. Whether it's the dark cold depths of heart break, the levitating feeling of being in love, the emptiness of being left behind, or how it feels to conquer and be triumphant, it ignites something inside. The longer you live the more you will adapt and overcome, but every degree of feeling is worth expressing.

Welcome, I am Rapheal De'Angelo. I am a Writer, an Actor, and Performer from Chicago. Art is my expression, here is my reality.

"I cheated on her heart with her mind. She said, it's fine.
As long as you love me and think of me at the same time."

Table of Contents

Momma 6	If You Only Knew 30
The Red Pill 7	Father and Son 32
My Kind of Woman 8	Hope You're Watching 34
If I Could 9	To: Love, From: Life 35
Imagine That 10	Decisions 36
Sound of Love 11	Fighting A Dream 37
Perfect Passion 12	Officially Done 38
Indeed 13	Battles of Intuition 40
Move through You 15	The Cycle 41
What Happened? 16	Awaiting 42
Dear Love 17	Women Say, Men Say 43
Unlucky 18	Damn I Miss You 44
Lie to Me 19	Between Our Stars 45
Not This Time 20	Surreal but Real 46
Me through You 21	Her 47
Wish It Was Real 22	This Is Love 48
True Love 23	Thank You 49
Pink Rain 24	Elated 50
Me and My Drink 25	Night To Remember 51
All in the Past 27	A Dads' Thing 52
Moments of Silence 28	Andre 53

Momma

Momma I see your eyes, I know you're crying

Your backbone is so strong you try to hide it

And these bills are piling up, they're getting higher

In a world that's so cold, I know you're tired

You go to work, sick as hell, you can't quit

You're on your own, 4 kids, and dad drifts

You hold it in but on this poem I'm going to vent

On a road, with no shade, I'll be your tint

So bet on me, I won't fail, I'll fix your problems

Your 2 cents plus my work, you have a dollar

You've done your part, you got us here through all the drama

So here's some wine, go unwind, I got us Momma.

The Red Pill

If life is a book, then why do we keep writing the same story
Society is a crook, stealing dreams and robbing glory
One question, Are you working or manifesting your blessings
A taste will have you craving for more than metrics could measure
If you want to see the world, stop orbiting the same street
The road to your desires, requires what ain't preached
How far you can go isn't dependent on where you are
It's something sown in your heart, it's embedded in your scars
The system isn't designed to supply you all you dreamed
Even degrees and diplomas won't guarantee life's ease
Dare to put action to passions, watch where it leads
Embrace the fear, let it fuel your ambition when you're on E
In this time that you're given, you're also given a choice
Blue is a quiet reality but The Red Pill brings the noise

My Kind of Woman

I love an adventurous, rebel, intellectual woman

God-fearing, strong minded, super sexual woman

Keep it classy, dash of sassy, a respectable woman

Call me daddy, make it nasty, unforgettable woman

Let him try it, she'll deny him, couldn't step to my woman

Never worry where she's at because she's next to me woman

If I Could

If I could I would crack the sky and spell your name with the stars.

If I could I would steal the sun and make shine wherever you are.

If I could I would touch your soul make you love me more.

If I could I would hold you close just open up your door.

If I could I would stop the time and erase the past.

If I could I would make every split second with you last.

If I could I would sneak into your dreams and save your day.

If I could I would be the one who takes your pain away.

If I could I would hold you while you cry until I drown.

If I could I would be the reason for your every smile.

If I could I would show you things that you won't believe.

If I could I would cherish you and give you all me.

If I could I would do all the things you ever wanted to do.

I swear to you I would, If I could be with you.

Imagine That

We can slow dance on the stars, our bodies' intertwined
Or cuddle on a cloud of passion that no one can find
As I gaze into your eyes and see dreams of us
A feeling grows inside paralyzing my mind, body and touch

In every single sparkle that your eyes project
It blinds all faults and all thoughts of regret
It's you who are my angel and my beloved goddess
Your needs I will please and till death I'll be honest

To possess your love and have it as mines to keep
For you, no sky's too high or no mountain's to steep
Visions of you and I, Just picture the sun rise
Where everyone's pain dies and tears you cry dry

Don't think open your mind, let me see what's inside
Are you feeling this vibe; so suddenly feelings climb
It's slowly moving your spine, it's like I wasn't alive
Since we met you've been like wings constantly taking me high

I love you beyond reason and I swear this isn't an act
I want to prove my emotions now try to imagine that

Sound of Love

See there's nothing I wouldn't do for you. Climb every mountain and search every sea too.

I would do it all just to be with you. Just to have you wrapped in my arms.

Like the paper on a Christmas present. I would wake up every morning.

Filled with joy and never sadness. With affection so intense I love you backwards.

Forward and even sideways. My love for you stretches further than highways.

The inertia of my love is everlasting. So capture this Kodak passion.

Let it grab you like the rapture. Because in this short life I feel like I'm that lucky bastard.

I will learn, you be the master. I will show up every day always on time.

To grasp every word you speak and make it mine. Your love is my sign of reason.

The weather of your divine eyes changes my season. My world comes to silence when you're breathing.

I'm overwhelmed by this feeling. A vibe so high the sky's my ceiling.

Physical, mental and spiritual healing.

Perfect Passion

I want to be so lost in you

I want to travel on the very imprints of your hands

I want to be able to reach and feel you

I want you to be mine and me your reflection

I want to only see you when I'm awake

I want to breathe your scent all in my air

I want to swim to the depths of your heart's lake

I want to blink and see moments we shared

I want to move to the beat of your heart

I want to feel the rise of your every smile

I want to be so close and never far

I want to hear the slightest whisper of your voice for miles

I want to be with you and that's all I'm asking

I want to have that feeling of Perfect Passion

Indeed

As slow as the sun rises her juices will fall.

So hollow like a bottle when I swallow her all.

She's flowing now dripping right down to my jaw.

My tongue is speaking her language. My lips just echoes it all.

Her body's talking back to me. My dick responds to her call.

I'm swimming into her lips. They grip as I hit her walls.

Now she's caressing my balls and I'm French kissing her neck.

Lick, nibble, and sucking I'm moving down to her chest.

Tongue mounding her breasts. Moaning losing her breath.

Ecstasy is the destination, I won't settle for less.

Great Passionate Sex is by far the best G.P.S.

So I follow directions, and put the bed to the test.

Damn we making a mess, but shit happens when it gets real.

Addicted to touching her body, no need for prescription pills.

Smoke her like Loud Cali Kush, ooh shit I love how it feel.

Getting high between her thighs then I eat it for real.

Pussy wetter than rivers I feel her tremble with chills.

I slide my dick deep up in her, stroking and kissing her still.

Body softer than silk, we switch position for me.

I'm going deep from back, she turn her head back to see.

Smacking her ass pulling hair I'm a hell of a freak.

Now she's throwing it back, got her reaching her peak.

I feel a rush as I'm thrusting, she's coming gripping the sheets.

She said, "Are you ready for more?" I look and tell her "Indeed."

Move through You

I'm driving on this road
Like I'm driving through your soul
But your eyes are my guide
So I'll never be alone

        I'm soaring through these clouds
        Like I'm soaring through your smile
        Every curve I will serve so
        I'll never see you frown

                I'm running through the rain
                Like I'm running through your pain
                The feeling of every drop
                Is like the whipping of a slave

I'm racing through the years
Like I'm racing through your fears
Every step I'm getting closer
To drying up all your tears

        I'm sailing cross this ocean
        Like I'm sailing through your emotions
        When all you need simply
        Is someone to show some devotion

                I'm jumping in this ride
                Like I'm jumping in your eyes
                To the bottom of your heart
                Where your forbidden feelings hide

I'm falling in this mud
Like I'm falling in your love
Now I'm covered in affection
So deeper and deeper I dug

        Like the air you breathe... I want to move through

What Happened?

What happened to the really cool, fun you

The girl guys would lie just to say they won you

What happened to big smiles and long laughs

When all we needed was you plus me, simple math

How'd we end up at everyday attitudes

Wake up early in the morning like I'm mad at you

How'd we let the little things start to get to us

Now we're checking calls and texts because we lacking trust

Is it time for us to go ahead and let it go

The right time to stay or leave, I'll probably never know

What's happened has happened, think we can get it back

We control the future baby, fuck the past

So can we make it last

Dear Love,

Suffocate is what I do when you're nowhere near me. I try to yell inside but the world just doesn't hear me. Look in my eyes and you can see the pain that I'm feeling. Don't try to count the tears that fall because it's in the millions. Now I'm sitting in the dark and I'm all alone. I'm on my hands, I'm on my knees, I'm praying you'll come home. Look me in my eyes and tell me that it's all okay. Lay your hand down on my heart and tell me, "I will stay." To feel your touch it does so much your lips I wish to kiss. The way you hold me tight and closely that is what I miss. If you knew the things you do and all that I would give. Just to hear you say the words, "I love you" once again. No kind of hurt, no such of pain could measure up to this. The way it used to be is why I love to reminisce. My heart is broke, hope is gone, and I feel that emptiness. Who dares to say that love is great I feel no happiness. I see the trap that most will end up falling in. It starts off perfect, feels so right but just wait till the end. He grows on her, she grows on him, and they both become so close. They laugh and flirt all through the night until their eyes are closed. They're so in love and try and say it every chance they can. Don't try and tell that I'm wrong because where you are I've been. The road gets tough, they're so confused, and they want to just give up. But yet they can't, and so they fight, because they care so much. Now things have changed, they have no choice, they have to just move on. Now you feel the way that I been feeling for so long… Alone.

P.S. I will always love you…

Unlucky

See I'm unluckily chosen. To feel the worst till I'm over. They say my heart is big and I say no it's beat up and swollen.
Laying out in the open. All smothered and choking. If it was up to me I'd leave it somewhere lost in the ocean.
Beat less and floating. Going nowhere fast, feeling like it's stuck in the moment.
Because my emotional motives are deep as ocean explores and the feeling that's growing the one made from your emotions is total control of my feet straight up to my shoulders.
Can't you see it you sowed it? I can feel it its holding, me back from everything I'd ever thought I'd get and I know it.
But I'm too scared to just show it. You got me down to my lowest.
Like an origami every single feeling is folding.
Sitting wishing that the silver lining of it was golden. Can't you smell it, it's potent? But not easily broken.
See if you ever hear me say, "Love you" out in open. If you do and you notice. I must be drunk and I'm smoking.
If you feel it when you read it think of me when I wrote it.

Lie To Me

She said,

Tell me that it's all a lie
Tell me that the rumors are wrong
Tell me that you wasn't with somebody else
Every time I was sitting at home
Tell me what we have is real
Tell me that our love is true
Tell me everything people said you did
That you didn't do

Tell me I'm crazy for accusing you
You thought that we had trust
Tell me that it really hurts you
Because, you care for me deeper than lust
Tell me when I looked through your coat
It only would make me feel better
Tell me when I washed that last load
That make up wasn't all on your sweater

Tell me when we talk on the phone
You're not texting someone else
Tell me when you went out last night
It was with friends or all by yourself
Tell me I'm the one you think about
Tell me it's me you adore
Tell me when I left your house at three
Nobody was coming at four

Tell me it's me you can't live without
Tell me that nothing will changed
Tell me these lies straight from your
Mouth, so I'll never feel the pain

Not This Time

The moment you realized what you

Created, you knew it wasn't art

And I wished it wasn't me.

Your smell was carried into my dreams.

I dreamt of many things, but you

You were something I'd wish to forget.

Instead you became a recurring truth.

A truth that provoked me towards you,

But we were never meant to be

And when you brought me to new places

You were never really there.

Your words are like lyrics I've heard before,

As much as I would love to listen,

Your song remains the same,

But I have changed…

Me through You

Drink my tears so you can taste my rain

Hold my soul so you can feel my pain

Meet my thoughts so you can know my mind

Fix my clock so you can change those times

Use my eyes so you can see my world

Search my life so you can find my girl

Steal my heart so you can sell my love

Take my arms so you can give these hugs

Hear my words so you can keep my secret

Me through you with some of my features

Wish It Was Real

Her sense of persuasion just grips your lips and sedates you

You'll wish this kiss isn't tainted with hints of imaginations

You feel it drip on your patience creating seas of temptation

And now the silence is broken provoking love at its greatest

The way she tends to this tension her body longs for attention

I give it every dimension of bliss till it flows consistent

I hear a whisper I listen and picture the most vivid visions

Passion surpassing my memories with deep devoted intentions

Got me pleading for more and needing emotions galore

Oh how I praise her amour it seeps down the depths of my core

Reeks with perfection of course my soul it yarns for her more

Behold the battle of affection she's the Goddess of war

Now these feelings are climbing so high we passed Mt. Olympus

From the way that this moment is growing its feeling endless

Witness this joy in my presence like presents opened at Christmas

The way we're sweating in minutes I get you wet with a quickness

So I might as well end this. Wish It Was Real...

True Love

True love never dies, it only lies dormant.

And it's always worth a fight even when you can't afford it.

So on the brink of giving up, remember why you started.

Because when you've had amazing, good and great become

    Disheartening.

Pink Rain

To sit and watch her, even from
A distance is a privilege
Her picture speaks far more
Than a thousand words
When she moves she levitates
On her own radiance
She holds the answers to questions
I haven't began to think of
Filled with wild wonder and adventure
Burdened with a heart of Gold
If I could be covered in one thing
And one thing only,
It would be Her Royal Highness's Pink Rain

(Not any Pink, Hot Pink)

Me and My Drink

My decisions in the beginning could have been better

That's why I'm sitting witnessing life in this cold weather

With no sweater, got my back to the wall

Pinned to the rim of sin by fear's rapture-like claws

My faults and my flaws. It's costing my all

Given the chance to do it again I'll probably say nah

I know it's ironic,

Going from girl to girl and saying it's strictly platonic

Got a hell of an addiction,

If she was going then I was going with her till I finish the mission

I was lost in a vision, I just wanted to kick it

You know, try to make a dollar, go out, and get some women

But never did I once try to break any hearts

Nor hurt any feelings because I'm still dealing with scars

Pressure from all directions it's best my mind is in the stars

Just me and this cup, sipping and drifting so far

But when indulge in this liquid medicine my thoughts release

Feeling the words I fail to speak, but I'm compelled to reach,

Reach for another taste of escape to place I often seek

Beholding the breakthrough of limits I couldn't breech,

And so I drink,

While it surges throughout my body I'm slowly levitating

Lifted into an abyss adjacent to where Heaven's gate is

In a realm where I prevail without all these complications

Now I'm one with this drink so I relax in its sedation

This is my meditation...

All in the Past

It's like I blink and think
A hundred days have gone pass
And then I see me breathe
Your memories right out the past

Why can't I sleep or eat
Without you running through my mind
Now I can hear you I feel you
You're sneaking up my spine

So I listen then picture
You standing right beside me
With that scent you sending
Got my senses growing, rising

Your perfect timing is surprising
I'm trying to comprehend it
Your presence is so familiar
Love when your spirit visits

I hate how all these moments
Get so real and then they're over
I'm overflowing with explosions
You're my supernova

Moments of Silence

In my moments of silence

My mind and soul opens like eyelids

Thoughts rush in like waves in the ocean,

Moved by strength and will of Poseidon

Deep in the caves that they hide in

I feel myself instantly dive in

I've been living but life isn't like this

I'm lost in a realm that is timeless

As the clock is slowly rewinding

I'm watching my sins intertwine in-

Side of my fears till they're bonded

Now I'm trapped in my own asylum

No control of this storm that I'm flying in

All alone when it strikes like lightning

In a zone that reveals what defines men

All my wrongs and my flaws seem to chime in

Picasso couldn't paint you this violence

Angels couldn't reach heights as high as this

These illusions intruding my conscious

So ruthless and fluent, why do they exist

It's chasing my sanity like vengeance

I'm praying for peace and repentance

My present just seems to reminisce

From yesterday back to my first kiss

I'm inhaling all of regret's stench

I'm wishing it all somehow made sense

I try reaching up for oxidation

Suffocated by life's complications

No medication and no meditation

While it charges with no hesitation

They say one true virtue is patience

What about when you're bare as a cavemen

No one's there when you're scared in your own skin

No sleep when it creeps in your place of Zen

Like nowhere you've been

A road without an end...

If You Only Knew

You see this music is soothing.
But the pleasure is only an illusion.
This mirage leaves you clueless,
Blinding your mind from finding where the truth is.

                    Never a second thought to step closer and see,
                    That I am not the person you proclaim me to be.
                                  I am not this smile,
                    I'm the camouflage pain you can't conceive.

Nor am I that joyous burst of laughter, you've grown to know.
I am the suppressed screams from continuously yelling no.
I dare you to look in my eyes and stare till your lids begin to strain.
If you really want to know me, I'll lend you some of my pain.
But it's not the kind that purges for hours it's the type to rest and leaves a stain.
Then wakes and grows stronger like an infection surging throughout your veins.

  You swear you know me. Is it because I walk with my head to the sky?
  Let me tell you a secret, promise to keep this between you and I.
    It's only up for one reason. I'm trying to stay alive
Thoughts of where I might go because any moment I'm planning to die.

Please tell me you understand. Like you've spent nights sleeping in dirt.
Make me believe the lies right from your mouth, I was born to hurt.
I wonder what you truly think of me. Maybe that I have everything, the works.
As if money brought happiness, and somehow it cures you when you're cursed.

    But like all humans we arrive here the same way then embark on separate paths.
    Through the depths of pain, stress, and obstacles I still will arise from this ash.
    I am these battles scars that unequivocally illustrates my triumph over my past.
    So, hello nice to meet you, because you clearly are familiar with only a mask.

You see this music is soothing.
But the pleasure is only an illusion.
This mirage leaves you clueless.
Blinding your mind from finding where the truth is…

Father and Son

Lord who am I and what's my purpose.

To do my will and leave my servants.

Lord I just can't plus, I'm not even saved.

Don't tell me you can't because I know what I made.

I still don't understand why did you pick me?

Lean not to your own understandings but in all your ways acknowledge me.

But I just met you why didn't you pick one of the first?

The first shall be last, and the last shall be first.

Just look at my life, God I'm not even worthy.

I prayed once or twice, but I didn't think you heard me.

I see all and hear all and yes I know what you did.

I was with you everywhere you went every time every sin.

Teach me how to repent and can you heal my spirit?

I want to know you like my favorite song, every note, every lyric.

When I wake I hear it. When I move I bare it

Make it the gift that never ends so I can go and share it.

Yea, though I walk through the valley of the shadow of death, I will fear no evil.

Because I know you died on the cross for me and all your people.

But Lord why do you love us so, when you know we don't deserve it?

For you are my children and much more than just my servants.

Hope You're Watching

This hasn't been getting eas**I**er since you've been gone
For some reason I thought time heals, guess I was wrong

My nights are **S**eeming longer from the chill of your side
Your smell's in the aroma but I can't fe**E**l your vibe

Our blood made us clos**E**, but life kept us together
I grew cold from obstacles, but you sent fire from heaven

Memories bring enemies, but I remember **Y**ou more
No kin to me, no need t**O** be, I can vouch for your core

My significant other, family, or j**U**st a friend
I hope you're watching me, can't wait to see you again

To: Love
From: Life

Let me start by saying I'm sorry I don't always turn out how you expect me to.
Sometimes, I cause pain which in turn makes them think less of you.
But why don't they see the value in us both, we are only gifts from him.
Instead they fight over money and power that only appeals to man.
What about of the soul, passion, and time? Are these not intangible enough?
When will they realize their purpose is not trapped by one sense but of the sum?
Not by years but by the days in each one. Not by this world but when it's done.
Why does it take battles to learn this war is never won? Maybe this is what they want.
But let's focus on all the good times we can and never let them go.
Because without you I have no point and without me you have no home.
So when you work your magic, I'll make sure that we are appreciated.
And in that moment they'll praise us both and know why they were created.

Yours Truly,
Life

Decisions

A match doesn't ask to be burned

A lesson doesn't ask to be learned

It's either you're last or you're first

I learned coming last leaves a burn

A heart doesn't ask to be broken

A sorry doesn't ask to be spoken

It's either you love or provoke it

Forgiveness hurts more when it's over

You make the decisions that teach you,

Burn you, break you, and heal you

Just decide to forgive yourself and others

That's how you keep moving forward…

Fighting a Dream

It's like I'm fighting a dream.

Wondering why I keep foreseeing this wonderful thing.

What does this mean? Is it just a dream?

I'm living inside of this fantasy world.

Trying to make it reality while I'm waiting for her,

But I don't know if I'm ready. Because I keep forgetting,

The way I used to be so nice, romantic, and all.

I'm trying to find that guy to give to her but I have evolved.

Don't even know what I am, nor what the hell I've become.

I've ignited a flame. It's burning up like the sun.

Confusion is conclusive when I think of her vibe.

Meanwhile, I aimlessly still search far for that guy.

But he's nowhere in sight. And I'm covered in darkness.

This tunnel's not looking bright, but her love is so harmless

I'm shaking my head trying to figure it out.

What I'm thinking doesn't match what's coming out of my mouth.

But yet I have to get rest. When that happens I start to dream.

And it all happens again a sick recycling thing. It's like I'm fighting a dream.

Officially Done

I just got pissed off

Listening to my grandma who's in love with a send off

Hearing how she sold her heart and kept getting ripped off

I'm trying to understand how a person can take so much

So I asked,

"How can you have the power to change it all and still fuss?"

She said God said forgive and you shall be forgiven

I was like "Okay well forgive, move on, and keep living."

When she told me she gets lonely I looked into her eyes

I could see the pain and even the nights she would cried

Anger grew inside made me want to find him and kill him

But I can't because I know she couldn't bare more than she's feeling

Worst part is my momma going through things too

She fall in love quicker than people catch the winter flu

She told me she just wants somebody that she can hold

Because she been lonely ever since my father left the home

Different guys coming over, she's trying to find a husband

Most were pathetic the others gave hope but kept running

I'm sick and tired of seeing my momma crying and hurt

Having her text them all day wondering where they were

I guess that's the problem with my family and me

We wear our heart on our sleeves for the world to see

But I'll be the one to change it all, understand me

No longer will I be the same old passionate me

No sweetheart, you can't get the time of the day

And all thoughts of me being affectionate I threw them away

Don't even look forward to me saying that four letter word

Because it's dead to me like fossils buried in the earth

I'm afflicted by this addiction I had with love

Well hello and goodbye to rehab I'm back to simpler drugs

Replacing kisses and hugs with liquor and popular clubs

No more looking back at that life I seen exactly what it does

I'm officially done.

Battles of Intuition

The more I tell her I'm not the more she tell me I am
The more I tell her I can't the more she tell me I can
Then she pulled it out her chest and put her heart in my hand
From the start I had some doubts I knew she couldn't understand

But I tried to be the better me she seen deep within
Being monogamous isn't easy with promiscuous friends
Pops said to thine self I should always be true
So to hell with what's expected, I do what I do

What is right in other's eyes didn't quite make the picture
Just 'cause you're sweet, smart, and sexy don't mean I'll be with you
Or when you're gone I won't miss you
Damn I wish things were different

Many pieces to a puzzle, one can keep it unfinished
Got more traffic of baggage then bags packed into planes
I guess I'm trying to keep my past way in the back of my brain
How could I ever let go when I'm still dangling from strings

I'm a fool but like Red Bull her smile keeps giving me wings
Now it's no stars in this sky maybe it's time to move on
Never got that One Wish maybe it's time to change songs
What if the feeling is right but ultimately it's wrong

Incandescently the love in me been shining so long
But they'll never see the best of me on regular basis
So those occasions when I spare a glance hold it and save it
Focus a picture and take it. Mold it, fold it like paper

This inconsistency inside me you'll need it for later
Never was good being patience, man I hate fucking waiting
So I'm out in these streets, my mind's off to the races.

This shit is crazy…

The Cycle

Been spending time with "Right Now"

I think she's falling in love

But I'm barely affording seconds,

"My Ex" keeps using them up

We still be missing each other

"Right Now" is probably "The One"

Too bad they don't have a clue

Their time is about to be done

'Cause "Dream Girl" has me trapped

I swear she's all that I need

I sent "My Ex" and "The One"

A text like, "I have to leave."

She got my heart in her hand

And I have never loved harder

Later I seen them together

She said, "Hi, my name is Karma."

Awaiting

I'm awaiting the moment when I say "Baby I changed."

And my actions will show it so I don't have to explain

I'm awaiting the moment my love takes your breath away

Then I'll give you all of my air until I nourish your veins

Just awaiting the moment when my eye sight is fixated

Distractions no longer capture my vision, it's automated

Yes, I'm awaiting the moment till I can only see you

And the likes become "Love you's" and "Love you's" turn to "I do"

I'm tired of waiting, losing my patience, when will it change

Feeling hopeless, notice time is lasting longer than pain

Damn waiting for moments of bliss and things unexplained

Because my emotional notions are dripping out of my brain

Drunk with anticipation for this moment I'm awaiting

The arrival of such, is more than dreams could've created

Now I'm just awaiting the moment when my waiting is over

So I sit, I think, and I wait for this closure

Women Say, Men Say

Women say they don't lie, Men say they don't cry
But I just seen a liar wiping tears from her man's eyes

Women say they want love, Men swear that they tough
But he's phone kissing while she be texting his bro-ther

Women say they're not hoes, Men say they have those
But she's pregnant by her friend's man and he can't find the right hole

Women say they're a Bad bitch, Men claim they sell bricks
But she packs layers of make up on and he stays on the Dean's list

Women say they don't need us, Men say that they can't trust
But she's pissed when he's away as he hides the fact he's in love

Women should say they need men, Men should say they need them
But everyone's afraid to say what they really feel deep down in

But I won't...

Damn I Miss You

As I gather every scent she left behind
Imbedded in the threads of my sheets and pillow
I inhale all of her until I'm overly high
Her seducing sweet cinnamon smells so simple

When I capture every glance I stole from time
Between blinks my memories are played in ripples
Visually she literally immerges before my eyes
A resurrection is perfected like a candle's rekindled

While I record every sound she spoke or cried
From the moment she provoke her lips to tremble
Like a crescendo from a whisper her voice arise
Now I hear her so vivid and clearer than crystal

Then I remember every taste she rendered my tongue
When she engulfed my buds with her slippery middle
So I'm licking and kissing her body undone
And this taste is more realistic than my mental

Now I collect every touch she surrendered my skin
Her enchanted massage and damn how she handled my pistol
Her smell, that taste, her voice, pretty face I want it again
But getting it is my biggest issue. Damn I really miss you

Between Our Stars

There were so many out there,
But she was my favorite. She was my friend.
It was like her light made sense to my reason.
While others were moving and growing and changing.
She, she still held my attention, and began
To fuel my purpose I long searched for.
She was special. She didn't quite shine
Like the others nor did she move like them.
But she was such a sight to see.
So I mustarded up the courage to shoot across the sky hoping to get
Closer, but I didn't. Then I shot across again, but failed once more.
Right as I prepared for another go, slowly she crept closer.
It was as if we gravitated towards one another.
For the first time we saw each other. In that moment only she and I existed.
In a galaxy of our own. No comets. No planets. Not one star but us.
Even though we never touched our hearts danced hand in hand.
We were so near but the space in between our stars haunted us.
I've never felt so distant. But we basked in the warmth of our union
Drifting in possibilities as hot as the sun.
We looked right into each other's souls and smiled
For there lied our very own reflection
Then suddenly it was over. It wasn't just our galaxy anymore.
Stars shot all around us. Comets invaded planets
And we, we grew further apart.
It wasn't until she was again, a distant admiration that I realized.
I will never want to be anywhere else,
But in the space Between Our Stars…

Surreal but Real

No fortune or magic
No horse and a dragon
Just a voice full of passion
And a life full of action
But I'm done with that chapter
Now it's you that I'm after
I need you, I want you baby
Damn I have to have you
Steal a star if you ask it
And the moon you can have it
Don't just hear what I'm saying
Girl you have to grasp it
I'm done as soon as I grab you
Because your heart is a classic
Trying to find your love but
I'm stuck in emotional traffic
Just hold on and fasten
Up this is till death then after
No need to fear me hear me
Clearly my love is relaxing

Her

Her aspirations are captivating,
Stroking my mind call it mental masturbation.
Caressing my thoughts kissing my faults.
I'm so elated. She don't ask she take it.

Like it was out for the taking.
Shooting her love at my wall.
She broke it down to the pavement.
Took my fear and just ate it.

Fixed my dreams and created,
A sense of bliss is just a risk
For me that's too complicated.
But her rapture of passion captured my imaginations.

I'm feeling sedated, my feelings inflated,
Waiting for the realness of reality
To kill it and take it.
So I sit and I'm waiting,

But this feeling ain't changing.
It's racing all throughout my head,
And this vision aunt fading.
Maybe it's real and I've made it.

So deep that I can't explain it.
Her kiss, her hugs, her touch,
Her love so much that I can't contain it.

This is Love

For my heart praises the whisper of her voice.

Engulfed in her perilous love I can only rejoice.

Her heart's as fragile and gentle as a cloud's soul.

More aberrational than the Leo Da Vinci code.

The mere attempt to abstain from her canny spell,

Is simply foolish and in that thought I dare not dwell.

Like the courage of a warrior I thrive through her fearless spirit.

I emulate no man who knows not the song of Love's lyrics.

Constantly I hear it. The burden of passion I beg to bare it.

Compassion I swear it. The more adversity I'll tear it.

I'll take her heart on a journey of jubilation.

With all that I have I'll shield her from tribulations.

I long to be the one who at her will happily surrenders.

This gift I wish to give to her shall always be remembered.

Between her kisses of bliss to the sincerity of my every hug,

I submit and commit entirely to her because THIS... IS... LOVE.

Thank You

She spoke with conviction
She laughed with beauty
Lost in awe when she's present
I keep pondering how she escaped
When did he notice she was gone
I know he wants her back
But I can't let her go
She's my air and I'll suffocate without her
So Lord I ask, allow me to hold on to your Angel
I don't know how long I have here
But I promise to be her wings when she falls
And with your help I will protect her
Every moment she remains on this earth
Thanks in advance

Elated

For we were madness in a world all too calm.

Where they deemed chaos,

We manifested our love

And in that instant I was doomed

Doomed to never love a smile other than yours

I've never loved more than the serenading sound of my heart

Beating in the palm of your hand,

One knows no equal and nor shall I ever.

It was the kind of elation that marinates in your soul

We felt the texture of forever

And once we grasped its warmth

It grew like wild fire and consumed

What you used to be reality…

Night to Remember

Your lips upon mines. My hands on your spine.
Just touching never lusting, but affection in mind.
And the tension inside, so quickly it climbs
To peaks never reached only dreams could find.
The temptation's amazing for so long I've waited.
You and I, all alone in this moment we created.
I give and you take it, no clothes bare naked.
We become one because it's love that we're making.
Pleasing yours needs is my only task.
So I give my all like this night is my last.
I do as you ask, anywhere anything.
While I'm stroking your body every time I go deep.
Your juices are flowing your wetter than seas.
You're coming like streams from the bed to the hall.
In the mist of the moment it's my name you call.
Just us and 4 walls witness this happen.
This time may have ended, but this feeling's everlasting.

A Dads' Thing

There's 10 fingers, 10 toes, 8 pounds and 6 ounces

You smile, "It's a boy" the doctor proudly announces

Questions storm my mind as you nestle in my arms

What if I fail to catch you when you trip and break your heart

When you fall and get a scar, to be a man when things are hard

To teach you, life isn't fair, so beware and trust in God

What steps do I follow to groom a son to praise a lady

Let her know that she's amazing, show her love, prove it daily

Now I'm watching you reach up, to hold my hands tighter

No surprise, you're like your mother, so strong and even wiser

I can tell you're a fighter, it's written all in your eyes

I only hope I can be a father worthy of you as my prize

My meaning of life…

Andre

You might've had a father, but I have a dad
Give his life just to give us what he didn't have

You might've known a guy, but I come from a man
You raised 3 boys, 2 daughters, and even our friends

Yeah he toughened us up, and he strengthened our minds
I was taught life's rough, you have to double your grind

You said not everyone will like you and it's okay
Love God, be respectful, and just let them hate

And I get why you left, I guess y'all grew apart
I was mad when I was young, but I know your heart

So when you're not around, I know you're out there working
Life's a trip but I don't fall, and Pops you're the purpose

www.ingramcontent.com/pod-product-compliance
Lightning Source LLC
Chambersburg PA
CBHW032102040426
42449CB00007B/1160